In the Memory
of David

In the Memory of David

R.J. Pommarane

Sunfyre Books, LLC

First Printing: 2015

ISBN: 978-0-9903709-5-6

Sunfyre Books, LLC
PO Box 12024
Portland, OR 97212

Cover Art courtesy of Pixabay.com
Author Website: www.rjpommarane.com

This book is dedicated with love to
Marvin "David" Brew
January 26, 1948, to December 7, 2014.

You will always be with me…

Table of Contents

Preface..1
Rocks *[free verse]*..................................3
True Faith *[haiku]*..................................4
Within the Circle *[story poem]*......................5
Don't Worry *[pantoum]*...............................7
Shaman *[sonnet]*.....................................8
The Value of Life *[pantoum]*.........................9
Cinematic Extraordinaire *[free verse]*.............10
Men *[free verse]*...................................11
Druid *[haiku]*......................................13
Alive *[sonnet]*.....................................14
Rosy-Colored Glasses *[story poem]*.................15
The Truth According to David *[sonnet]*............17
I Am He *[free verse]*...............................18
Have No Fear *[free verse]*..........................19
Taboo *[pantoum]*....................................21
Sinking Steps *[sonnet]*.............................22
Tanqueray and Tonic *[story poem]*..................23
Vines *[haiku]*......................................25
French Protestant *[free verse]*....................26
Seeds of Emotion *[free verse]*.....................27
Widower *[haiku]*....................................29
Avalon *[sonnet]*....................................30
Waters All Around *[free verse]*....................31
Sunday Night *[free verse]*..........................33
Quiet Voice *[free verse]*...........................34
Liberal Enterprise *[story poem]*...................35
Twins *[haiku]*......................................37
Sisters *[free verse]*...............................38

Sixteen Percent *[free verse]*...........................39

Echoes *[pantoum]*.....................................41

Double-Edged Sword *[sonnet]*.....................42

Etched in Stone *[free verse]*........................43

Knowing *[haiku]*......................................45

The Universe *[pantoum]*...........................46

Damn Republicans *[story poem]*...................47

Rising *[haiku]*..49

Graying *[sonnet]*......................................50

The Children *[story poem]*..........................51

Desires *[pantoum]*....................................53

Communal Thought *[haiku]*........................54

For the Love of a Mother *[free verse]*..............55

Early Mornings *[story poem]*.......................57

Pinterest and Twitter *[story poem]*................59

War *[haiku]*...61

Goodbye *[free verse]*.................................62

Episcopacy *[story poem]*.............................63

Freedom *[haiku]*......................................65

Volcanoes *[sonnet]*...................................66

The Wise Man *[free verse}*...........................67

Preface

The death of my closest friend in this life came as a devastating loss, driving me into a paralyzing period of unyielding grief. I couldn't imagine life without his guidance and reassurances. I often wonder if the grief might've been lessened if we'd more time to process the severity of David's diagnosis but there was no time. He was diagnosed with cancer in October of 2014 and by December 7, 2014, he was gone. Ten excruciating weeks of pain and psychotic delusions were all we were given to say our goodbyes. It wasn't enough.

The morning after David died, as I was consumed by tears of overwhelming sadness, I pulled out my notebook and started writing. I wrote *Have No Fear* that day and the process made me feel better. I continued writing at least one poem every day and, as the words flowed onto the paper, my grief continued to lessen. When I would sit down in my chair and write these poems, I thought about what David would do and say if the situation had been reversed, if I had passed away and he had remained alive. I know he wouldn't stop living. He would take a devastating event and extract from it any positivity he could ascertain and use it to instill happiness in others. David enjoyed writing and he loved reading my work. I know he would've encouraged me through every step of this process. He would've enjoyed these poems.

David always encouraged my passion for the English language. I devoted seven years of my life to the pursuit of classical training in literature and advanced degrees in English. David was there every step of the way, quietly encouraging me to reach for the stars and overcome all obstacles in my path. He was an avid fan of my formal training and urged me to write poems in the classical forms, despite my passion for the composition of prose poetry.

One of my great regrets is that I didn't heed his request and compose poems in the formal poetic forms while he was still living. However, in his memory, this entire collection is a composite of five classical poetic forms. Each poem is about David or is inspired by David's beliefs. I present this collection to the world as an homage to the life of David Brew and in gratitude for all his support and love. You're immortal now, my dear friend, held forever imprinted upon these poems, for all the world to see and know you.

I wish more than anything he was still here with me but I take great comfort in knowing how much powerful love and inspiration still exists in the memory of David...

Rocks

His love of rocks was unique
They were jewels for him to seek.

Rocks of all shapes and sizes
In all different hues and guises

Each rock he gave a different name
They were his fortune and his fame

They were the greatest thing to him
He would talk rocks on a whim.

For David it was plain to see
Rocks held power and energy.

He placed each rock on display
And when asked he would say:

"Nothing on this earth is ever forsaken
One day all these rocks will awaken."

True Faith

The law of god says
That true faith is not written.
It lives in the heart.

Within the Circle

In his daily life he was only a man but when he stepped within the Circle he became a master of the magic of the soul. Upon rooting his feet over the threshold of the broom he would rise up like a genie released from his lamp to grant an unsuspecting spectator a single wish. He was a sage, bearing the mark of secret wisdom passed through generations since the days of the druids in the rites of the ogham. Oaken was his staff, with a wreath of holly upon his brow. His spirit was that of a peace-filled sorcerer bent upon using magic only for the purpose of common good.

The more he looked upon the world from within the Circle, the greater he came to know himself. He taught others the power of humility but, in himself, maintained the veracity of a priest or politician. Quiet tongues were his tribute, silently enthralled by his many faces shifting in the smoke of the fire burning on the middle altar in offering to the gods. Hiding beneath a hooded cloak of black velvet did nothing to reduce the brilliance of his spirit light. It only intensified the astonishing qualities of his basic earthen nature.

In one hand he held an orb of water and in the other a wisp of air. His eyes beamed like precious rubies reflecting the light and his smile, his smile shined with the light of the sun. He embodied the great Kernos of the forest-dwelling satyrs in his whimsy and his wisdom but his strength was that of the Dagda, the rising son of the sun-father of the Tuatha de Danann. His was a countenance that drew upon the whimsical powers of the fae. He called all manner of men to his side in his quest to continue the traditions of our Briton ancestors, to expound upon the principles set forth by the long dead high masters of the burning Forest House.

He knew in life that, when we die, our spirit rises from our ashes to endure the long voyage across the Lake of Mists and into that Otherworld from whence we were all born. He was the acolyte to the King of Kings under the banner of the red Pendragon. All the roots of his blood were bound to the men of the west, those of the Britons, those of the Burgundians, those of the Franks. His was a countenance of the old ones, the ancients that came before us, the descendants of Atlantis. Prince Rur Aniok the Blessed.

This quiet, gentle man with a penchant for sparking conversations and revitalizing the spirit of others was only the outward image of a great and glorious mage wielding ancient magic seen only as a secret within the Circle.

Don't Worry

Don't worry.
The sky will not fall because I am gone
Your heart will not cease its beating and
The sun will continue rising every day.

The sky will not fall because I am gone,
Though it may feel like your world is breaking.
The sun will continue rising every day
Even if it feels you've descended into darkness.

Though it may feel like your world is breaking
It is only the process of your massive grief.
Even if it feels you've descended into darkness,
Your respite in the shadows will be fleeting.

It is only the process of your massive grief
Bringing you to fall breathless to your knees.
Your respite in the shadows will be fleeting
A return to living is practically guaranteed.

Bringing you to fall breathless to your knees
Is the idea that you will never fully recover but
A return to living is practically guaranteed.
Don't worry.

Shaman

Whenever it was his distinct pleasure
He'd shroud himself in a magic cowl
And take flight to seek wisdom's true treasure
In the full white form of a snowy owl.

At other times he would sprout a blue fin
And seek out deep seawater at a whim,
Where the hand of mankind has never been,
In the kingdom where the gray dolphins swim.

Greatest of all is when he'd grow taller,
Bearing a snout and long, matted black hair,
Around him normal people grew smaller
As he assumed the visage of a bear.

He lived his whole life in the twelfth hour,
Destined to possess shamanic power.

The Value of Life

The value of life cannot be measured
In terms of gold, rubies, or silver.
It can only be judged upon the altar of
Merit through earthly action and deed.

In terms of gold, rubies, and silver
Men can allow their minds to be clouded.
Merit through earthly action and deed
Can no longer be practically achieved.

Men can allow their minds to be clouded
By selfish thoughts where enlightenment
Can no longer be practically achieved
Without intervention by the divine.

By selfish thoughts where enlightenment,
Banished from the sphere of intelligence
Without intervention by the divine,
Becomes the embodiment of reasoning.

Banished from the sphere of intelligence,
Men creep back to when the ultimate answer
Becomes the embodiment of reasoning:
"The value of life cannot be measured."

Cinematic Extraordinaire

He was a connoisseur of the silver screen
There was no movie he had not seen
No cinematic space he had not been.

From the days of Astaire to the days of Pitt
He could name every actor with any wit.
By the love of movies he had been bit.

Every film held its secret appeal
Their messages he could feel
Whether set realistic or surreal.

About each movie he showed great care
He was a font of wisdom with a name to bear
As the one and only Cinematic Extraordinaire...

Men

He always watched them as they walked by
Especially if they were young and firm.
The redheads especially caught his eye
He'd become like a bird chasing a worm.
As he silently pursued his latest pleasure
He would watch them closely from afar
Like he was a pirate and they his treasure
A valuable trinket at an antique bazaar.
This was the game he would always play
A graying brown fox stalking his prey…

If the young man decided to approach
He would flirt, and laugh, and talk
On his honor he would never encroach
Like a gentleman on a courting walk.
If the man showed interest he'd ramp it up
He let his lusty intentions be known.
Like a priest drinking from the holy cup
His seeds were prepared to be sewn.
The fields were ploughed and ready
A farmer holding his oxen steady…

There was another side to his charm
A voyeuristic envy he often dreamed
Of intense exchanges absent real harm
With men who were not what they seemed.
He had a taste for the edgy, hot young one
His eyes would betray a deep hidden lust
Like clouds parting to reveal a red sun
Or the peaceful reprieve of settling dust.
He drove himself to the edge of the earth
An eager mother about to give birth…

Beneath all his ever congenial bluster
There resided a kind natured bard.
Never beguiled by young, false luster
Willing to play his last wild card.
There were always men who drew his eye
But there was only one he called his own.
He could never explain exactly why
The truth in his heart was shown.
In his life there had been one, not two,
A single love that he held to be true...

Druid

Druids in the sun,
Draped in cloth of silver white,
Silently knowing.

Alive

There was once a time when he was alive
And things felt like they'd forever be the same.
He was always meant to thrive and survive
Not be prematurely thrown from the game.

His vigor was mighty, his soul was strong,
He was alike to the holy white dove.
His spirit free to forgive any wrong,
A prodigal son born from divine love.

Alas, he had but few years left to live
His hidden flame burned intensely too bright
In a world that took all he had to give
Before it drowned out his exquisite light.

Blessed priest of the goddess of the moon
An aged pagan pilgrim gone far too soon.

Rosy-Colored Glasses

When I first met David, I was an angry person. I was angry all the time and he, he shined like a ray of light. He was my ailing grandmother's dearest friend in her last days and showered her with all his kindness. As I descended into my final battle with my demons, he stood vigil, like a pious pilgrim guarding the road to the holy city of Jerusalem.

Even after I won my battle, I remained a bit of a cynic. I was the realist who values pragmatism above passion. David chided me for my abrupt uneasiness concerning the fate of mankind and the restoration of the powers of earth. He would tell me that "all things under the sun are born equal and each deserves respect." He was no fan of eye for an eye and abhorred punishment in all its forms. In those days, I was a different man, one who saw the validity of taking a human life if that human was convicted of a heinous crime. I saw the ends as justifying the means. I was a registered Republican. David touched my heart and reignited my dormant passions. He used his divine knowledge of the world and its many secrets to drown the darkness rooted in the deep parts of my spirit so that I might rise up like the phoenix reborn from its ashes. He became my teacher and brought me to stand with silent wisdom.

As my passion became my principle, my heart lightened. I no longer endorsed martial punishment. I no longer used anger as a weapon. Yet I still remained a realist. Where others might see a spark of hope and still others would assume the situation to be empty, I saw it exactly as it existed. David came to accept my outlook, though he remained adamantly against any truth that did not resonate with his peaceful energy. His was a power that only worked when the heart was full of love. He wore rosy-colored glasses that transmuted the darker aspects of living into a pleasing and gentle hue. He only saw the good in others.

David was always present in the present. His dominion was the hearts of the free feeling folk. Those whose hearts were filled with the light of the loving spirit of the Creator. David, even though you have moved on to the next world, I will continue to cherish your teachings in honor of your soul. Your rosy-colored glasses have found a new home.

The Truth According to David

David believed in the goodness of man,
That every soul is born innocent.
People are destined to do what they can
To ensure all their goodness isn't spent.

We all choose our road, either right or wrong,
And must live with the effect of our choices.
We each compose our own personal song
Which gives rise to our limitless voices.

No strong willed person should hesitate
To defend others, or to make a stand.
We are obliged to rise and meet our fate
As the god and goddess have always planned.

The truth according to our David Brew
Was being kind is being true to you.

I Am He

Dancing in the ethers at the dawn of time,
Singing the songs of creation.
Thought becomes sight, touch, and smell
As his senses start to awaken.

He hears voices rising from across the veil
Asking for divine absolution.
They speak of lust and weakness of will
Leading towards temptation.

Of hunger and pain, war and disdain
The flaws in the human design.
In sorrow and shock, their hearts hard as rock
Chaos clouds the signs.

A problem arises as he sits with the stars.
While he possesses sight beyond sight
His ears are muffled by the ethereal sounds
Echoing from the cosmic light.

He wonders at the words piercing his mind
And he speaks aloud to those he can't see:
"They call for God and I find it odd they think
I am he."

Have No Fear

You told me once to have no fear,
To follow my inner voice.

You said you'd be there to hear
And guide my every choice.

In many ways you were my father,
My teacher, my only friend.

I never thought I'd see the day
Our time would come to an end.

My heart broke a little when you left
I felt like I didn't say goodbye.

It hurt too much to smile and
It hurt too much to cry.

Then you reached across the darkness
From the world of the grave.

You touched me on the shoulder
All my trespasses you forgave

You whispered that you loved me
That I had been your truest friend.

And I told you I love you too
Always and without end.

Then you vanished into the wind
Leaving me with my grief.

Instead I felt your blessings
I was filled with relief.

There is but one last thing to say
And then all will be done and through.

I will walk the path you set for me
With the kindness I learned from you.

Until my road comes to an end,
My dearest friend, I fondly bid you adieu.

Taboo

He said no subject was ever taboo.
All things were topics for conversation
In the nighttime when we sat and thought
About all the hurts and woes of the world.

All things were topics of conversation.
Politics were at the forefront of the issues
About all the hurts and woes of the world
And the penultimate suffering of man.

Politics were at the forefront of the issues
David discussed with his friends and family.
And the penultimate suffering of man
Was a subscript of his oratory platforms.

David discussed with his friends and family
That the principle conviction of his inner heart
Was a subscript of his oratory platforms
Existing as an extension of his beautiful soul.

That the principle conviction of his inner heart
Shined out from deep within his radiant mind.
Existing as an extension of his beautiful soul,
He said no subject was ever taboo.

Sinking Steps

A human life is extremely fleeting,
It passes in the quick blink of an eye.
One day the frail heart simply stops beating,
Our breath leaves us with a guttural sigh.

Life comes and goes, it waxes and it wanes,
Nothing in this world goes on forever.
The sacred principle the earth sustains:
Death comes for all, rich, poor, dumb, or clever.

The point is not the end of the journey
It's about the sights seen along the way,
About every unbridled yearning
On the unending quest to seize the day.

Knowing that all the things wrought by our hand
Are sinking steps imprinted in the sand.

Tanqueray and Tonic

David was never much of a drinker. He was fairly straight-laced when it came to his personal vices. He liked to eat, maybe a little too much, and he watched a lot of television but alcohol was beyond his indulgences on nearly every occasion. He only had a drink when we went out dancing.

David would dig his heels into the dance floor and affect his own unique brand of movement. The only way I found the courage to dance was to imbibe endless amounts of alcohol but David could move freely and uninhibited in his natural state of mind. His character was forever undiminished and his honor instilled in his courage, a courage to stand on a dance floor full of twenty year olds and shake his moneymaker as though he had not a care in the world. I think about his lack of inhibitions regularly, pondering what mechanism existed within his mind to allow him such freedom. I know he was a self-conscious person by nature and his self-esteem was not always the best, so he had to derive the strength to dance from some other place, an unseen energy stored within the layers of his aura, projected by the glorious white light of his inner spirit.

In truth, I've never been that outgoing, though my mind has always been sharper than the katana of a samurai. It this David and I were unalike. His mind was dulling with the onset of his golden years but he was the most exuberant individual I've ever known. His tongue was silver and his words were gold. He brought a smile to every face. His moves were a mixture of comedy and tragedy. He would dance the night away and stay as long as we were able. I often retired before he did. I'm a little overweight and a lifelong smoker so my breath would leave me with very little effort. In the first days of our friendship, David was lithe and had no addictions. At more than twice my age, he had more stamina in his left hand than I had in the whole of my body. Eventually, his strength waned and his periods of dance became shorter but he always maintained his joyful disposition and headed to the floor whenever possible.

David was never much of a drinker. A few times I saw him have one or two beers, and another time a Rum and Coke, but these events were rare. To gather his strength, David required only one drink that he nursed all night and that drink was, almost always, a Tanqueray and Tonic with lime.

Vines

Alike to the heart
When left without attention,
Vines bear bitter fruit.

French Protestant

Anyone who saw you could tell at a glance
That your family heritage was not complex
Your people were once citizens of France
Under the lawful gaze of a tyrant Rex...

Yours were a people put to the test
In a war of Churches set on holy conquest.

On one side stood the House of Bourbon
On the other the duplicitous Guise
Who viewed reforms within the Church
As akin to a lecherous disease...

To France Luther and Calvin had brought
The answer for reform so many had sought.

Yours were on the side of those who'd be free
From the hypocrisy of the priesthood and
The ultimate power of the Roman See
Within the borders of your ancestral land...

With the blood of many slow freedom was bought
For the vigilantly protestant French Huguenot.

Seeds of Emotion

In the depths of your despair
You tried always to be fair.
And to teach me as you always had
That apathy can drive one mad.

More than any lesson you knew this thing
The words of the primal song we sing.
You were a teacher of highest accord
To die by the pen rather than by the sword:

There are certain things a man needs
Like water, food, and sleep.
Urges that drive their every deed
To sew, grow, then reap.

Another urge is the lust for sex
To couple in primal heat,
Unaware of unwanted effects
When man and woman meet.

Beneath the urges and needs of man
Rest the seeds of emotion.
Designing for each a master plan
Harnessing their devotion.

As important as the basic design
Comes the desire to grow,
To question, seek, and to find
That man should always know:

The lesson you told in your last days
In a way that for me will always amaze.
You opened up about your grief
And the greatest lesson in your belief:

The greatest human imperative
Is not to die before you live.

Widower

Widowers are free
To remember the best times
And forget the rest.

Avalon

Beyond the earth, through a gray veil of mist,
There lies the island of apples and oak.
A magic place where the dead still exist
And the living are the butt of the joke.

They dance by day but they lament the night
At the edge of their bright, translucent lake.
They guide souls to the universal light,
While seeing death as the cruelest mistake.

Souls become faeries that flit through the rain
To find the path back to the mortal day,
Measuring each loss and every gain,
Questing to return what death took away.

He has passed into the twilight, they say,
A new subject for the Queen of the Fae.

Waters All Around

Almost every Sunday morning
The three of us went out to eat.
Breakfast at Milo's or Cadillac
Always a delightful treat.
We'd be seated at the table
Quickly and without delay
You'd order coffee with cream
And ask the specials of the day.
You would listen intently with a smile
And had an aversion to those who frowned.
With a delightful gesture, you'd say
"Waters all around."

I could never understand why
You would order a water for me
When I never drank it, not once,
As you could plainly see.
I thought maybe you were
Saying I looked dehydrated
In your own special way you
Wanted my thirst to be abated.
You were always looking out for
Me and the people I respect.
Living up to your lasting ideal
To defend and to protect.

After you died I started thinking
Again, about your kind small action
To try and understand the meaning
Of your apparent satisfaction.
If it was not to be the father
To us youngsters, your dear friends

Than it was something else
Something with a finite end.
I think on some level you were
Sparing the rod and the knife
By reminding us that
Water is the source of all life.

Sunday Night

Sunday nights we spent in my place
Watching the Desperate Housewives
I loved to see the look on your face
When the wives brandished knives.

When our show came to its end
You were extremely saddened
Then we found Once upon a Time
And you were no longer maddened.

Our shows were our special time
To bond, to laugh, and to share
I would read poems made in rhyme
And you always showed you care.

For many years it was me and you,
Into our shows we would take flight
I looked so forward to pursuing
Each and every Sunday night…

Quiet Voice

There are men in this world who live in shame
With regret for all they have lost.
There are those who do anything to shirk blame
No matter the ultimate cost.

Then there are those who only give
And ask for nothing in return.
Their lives they quietly live
With bridges they never burn.

He was one of those kind of men
Living his life in quiet piety
He was absent any earthly sin
And he valued sobriety.

It was always his sacred choice
To live his life with a quiet voice…

Liberal Enterprise

Radically liberal does nothing to describe David's political outlook. He was a democrat in every sense of the word, fighting for the welfare nation and against the vehement oppression of the minorities in these our United States.

David saw suffrage for every man as the pinnacle of peaceful civilization. If ethnic and class barriers were to cease, men would have nothing left to fight about. The economics of the nation is centered on the drive of money to dominate the hearts of men and women alike. People have done worse than murder in the lust for wealth.

The only affluence David sought was one of philanthropic principle. He used to say the only reason he wished to be wealthy was so that he might provide for others who were of lesser means. The principle of the common nation ran through David's veins. He was against the ownership of powerful guns and saw topics built on platforms of morality as propaganda meant to distract from the real topics.

The budgetary concerns of the nation were the concerns of my dear friend. As the wealthy continued to hoard the riches of the nation and the government fell into financial disgrace, he turned his mind towards the injustices carried out by the elite. He despised those who sought to take and take while feigning they had nothing to give back. The middle-class began to vanish and only the white or blue collars remained. Like Buddha to the men of India, David wished to be associated with the white only to command others of affluence to lay down their proverbial arms and return control of the nation to those upon which its foundations were built. All men are meant to be the same.

By calling people to look inward through poignant conversation and prose, David meant to instill in us all the idea that our enemies should be met with compassion and not disdain. He was dedicated to the cause of the underdog and wished for everyone to be the same. Rather than calling his friends to arms, to face down their enemies with war or plague, he asked us each to engage in the peaceful but strong propagation of his new age liberal enterprise.

Twins

Twin souls keep loving
Far beyond the veil of death
As the stars above.

Sisters

His sisters were a blessing, he'd always explain,
A sweet ray of sunshine amidst heavy rain.

An older brother who bore the weight
Always ready to wash clean the slate.

He listened to them with bended ear
Endeavoring to make his opinions clear.

He gently guided them in their choices
Never chided or condemned their voices

A loving brother who used to gloat
Filial devotion is a book he wrote.

He never told me any unkind things
About either sister with angel's wings…

Sixteen Percent

You were obsessed with your phone
With how much energy would remain.
Would it be enough to function?
Would it be enough to sustain?
I don't know what you thought…

You watched the power fall away
Like a clock ticking down to zero.
You would plug it in to save its life
Like a strong, unsung hero.
Relief was always what you sought…

I never cared if my phone had power
As long as it worked without a delay.
And if it broke I would never fret,
I would just quickly throw it away.
At least that's what I'd been taught…

I never wasted my time on losses
I focused only on what I could gain
I thought your obsession so absurd
It brought you only stress and pain.
That phone bothered you a lot…

You spent your nights on the screen
Looking at this, this, or that
You drained its power steadily
Like a mouse falling to the stalking cat.
But you plugged it in at 16% on the dot…

At 80% you would start to shake
At sixty your discontent became known
At 40% your face would turn very red
At twenty your fears would be shown.
Against the drain you always fought...

The draining battery was a metaphor
For your fear of aging and death
By plugging in the fading battery
You tried to buy yourself another breath.
But a longer life cannot be bought...

Sooner or later all batteries
End up at zero percent.

Echoes

Echoes can be heard long after fading
If you place your ear near to the ground
You can still hear distant hearts breaking
Within the shadows and places of twilight.

If you place your ear near to the ground
You can hear his echo forever whispering
Within the shadows and places of twilight
Seen with the raw power of the third eye.

You can hear his echo forever whispering
Songs of splendor emblazoned with light
Seen with the raw power of the third eye
In small moments of absolute stillness.

Songs of splendor emblazoned with light
Sung to resist the inevitable end of all things
In small moments of absolute stillness
When others are silently dreaming.

Sung to resist the inevitable end of all things,
The spells of the spirits of the dead, knowing
When others are silently dreaming
Echoes can be heard long after fading.

Double-Edged Sword

Love for others can be the greatest gift.
It can heal the hurts of wounded nations.
It can close the gap in any wide rift
And give life to man's greatest creations.

All affection has a far darker side.
Caring can be as heavy as a cross.
Bearing the brunt of a turbulent ride,
Loving often leads to the ultimate loss.

If one can stand against impending grief
They may live their life as a hallowed saint
But if one is called to selfish relief,
Their soul is their own, to cleanse or to taint.

Give kindness as much as you can afford
Knowing that love is a double-edged sword.

Etched in Stone

The face and features of the body
Are not where the soul resides.
Beneath his skin, deep within,
Something different hides.

By day he is a man of love
But at night he is full of sin.
He washes in regret and guilt
Trying to remember when.

When life was so much better
Simple and without disdain.
Filled with youthful innocence
And pleasure without refrain.

He lost those happy feelings
Somewhere along the way
His life gave way to monotony
Boredom, every day.

His heart grew hard with sadness
And jealousy of all those who live.
He felt his spirit hardening and
He had nothing left to give.

His fate was etched into stone
When he turned to the other side.
The pestilence overwhelmed him
Until the night he died.

That destined night in his room
As he gasped to take a breath
He prayed that God would grant
To him a hasty, painless death...

Knowing

Find the peace in truth,
Knowing that all things that live
So too they must die.

The Universe

The universe is our maker,
The one who gave life to the cosmos.
The cosmos sustain us in all our dealings
Though we choose not to see the truth.

The one who gave life to the cosmos
Is the one who gave us the earth,
Though we choose not to see the truth,
Blinded by the pursuit of pleasure.

Is the one who gave us the earth
The same being who set us up to be
Blinded by the pursuit of pleasure
Regardless of the consequences?

The same being who set us up to be
Distracted by greed and selfishness
Regardless of the consequences
Made us to really be kind and giving.

Distracted by greed and selfishness
Man has forgotten who it was that
Made us to really be kind and giving.
The universe is our maker.

Damn Republicans

"I've had it with those damn republicans," David said when Boehner announced the archconservative intent to always filibuster legislation that could help to end the suffering rising amidst the poor of America. No man should have to suffer for the sins of another. It was his intent hope that the liberal mind would eventually come to rule the day.

When George Bush Jr. was elected President, David kicked a trashcan across the room. He cursed the suspicious way in which the election was called and demanded that justice be done. Shortly thereafter the twin towers fell and America declared war. David lamented the loss of the lives in the tragedy of 9-11 but he never once advocated eye for an eye. As other Americans called out for the blood of Muslims in retribution for their losses, David knew that violence begets violence. The cycle of destruction would continue and innocent blood would be forever spilled and children and women would be lost.

As the debt ceiling rose and any real resolution to the problem dissolved, David genuinely feared for the future of the United States. He saw the archconservatives and their constituency of elite as a malevolent malignancy causing the American people to slowly decay. The blame was placed squarely on the shoulders of the republicans for refusing to compromise in any way with their enemies across the aisle. As the tyranny of the Bush administration continued to unfold, David withdrew fully from any real association with those who bore a conservative mind.

David breathed a sigh of relief the day Obama and the liberals overtook the conservative supremacy and claimed power over the country by right of the people's vote. Then a new worry came. The republicans refused to relinquish their claim of absolutism and began the senatorial war. Each step taken back towards the conservative agenda was like a wound driven into David's heart with a spear. I saw him steadily become deflated, the long hope he held for the future of the people was waning towards its end.

At the last of his full life, David was left to wonder if his opinions had been heard, truly heard by the individuals he attempted to influence. These words, written this day, shall serve as testimony that he not only touched the lives of many, he instilled into my heart the laws of liberalism.

Rising

Life is the spirit
Rising like a wave to drown
All adversity.

Graying

In the beginning, the world was new
And the stars shined brighter in the night sky.
From heaven the gods had a clearer view
Of men who are born and destined to die.

As the new earth grew steadily older,
There came to the planet the race of men
Who started meek but grew ever bolder,
Reveling in dark temptations and sin.

The cosmos are now exceedingly old
And men live like a malignant disease.
Many souls of sinners are daily sold
In hopes that the burden of life will ease.

While monks, nuns, and priests are busy praying
All things under the sun are now graying.

The Children

Blessed is the innocence of children. It reminded jaded adults of the simpler days of their youth and of the small pleasures to be had if only we stop and take the time to see them. Each young heart is filled with wonderment brought on by the grandeur and undiscovered vastness of the world. When we are young we think life goes on forever and all things are the byproduct of some kind of unexplainable perfection. The young heart beats stronger and faster because it his filled with the awe of the nature and the depth of the world of imagination. They spend their days playing make-believe in forests with faeries or as pirates in distant Neverland. Before the dark reality of the world sets in, from parents telling their children to grow up or of harsh circumstances ravaging their souls, the young remain the embodiment of all the innocent. Youthful tears are pure.

David valued innocence above all things and cherished the time he spent with the children. He talked constantly of the young people in his life. Jordan and JC, his beloved nephews, Justice and Ehko, his adopted nieces, and the children of his sister's child, Matthew and Justin. All of them meant the world to him and he strived to keep constant updates on their activities and achievements. He loved to free his spirit and return to his youth, even if it was only for an hour or two. Whenever we would go to visit our friend Randi, he would run off and hang out with her daughter. They climbed trees, played hide-and-seek, and enjoyed some down time with Barbie. I've never seen an adult with such an avid spirit for engaging in activities to return to the innocence of youth. A nature fueled by kindness and sincerity led him to feel free enough to forget the confines of adulthood and find that place of pure youthfulness again.

Through all the hardships of life, all the barriers we must cross along the way, we can become beleaguered and the light of our soul diminished. The sadness of reality can rise up like a wave to wash away our hope and goodness. It is only when we stop to smell the roses and to play in the fields with the children that our power is returned and we remember we each create our own world in the depths of our perceptions. If we choose to be free than it shall be.

At least that's what David would say.

Desires

Desires are ingrained in every man,
Every person has dreams for the future.
The only obstacle to earthly desire
Is the question of our own self-worth.

Every person has dreams for the future
From a young and formidable age.
Is the question of our own self-worth
Born in those early days of living?

From a young and formidable age
We are set upon a road with two paths,
Born in those early days of living,
The choice to fulfill or ignore our desires.

We are set upon a road with two paths,
Forced to walk one way or another in
The choice to fulfill or ignore our desires
In a reality where people are often forgetting.

Forced to walk one way or another in
The race to fulfill our dreams before we die
In a reality where people are often forgetting
Desires are ingrained in every man.

Communal Thought

The communal thought
Is the samurai to fight
Against the selfish.

For the Love of a Mother

Every Sunday you spent with your mother
Who was in many ways your best friend
I know you never preferred another
You talked about her without end.
I think you would have missed her
If she had left this world before you
Life would have become a hazy blur
You would have been left nothing to do.
Your mother was your partner in crime
Your fellow, your admirer, your queen
The ruler of your heart for all of time
The truest relationship I have ever seen.

Yours was a bond that ascends the real
A quiet exchange of raw emotion
She was the catalyst to help you feel
The wholeness of your devotion.
It was the little things that made you smile
The laughs that you would exchange
A penchant for caring all the while
A cadence to show your full range.
You talked about your mother every day
And always showed familial pride.
She showed through in all your ways
When you laughed and when you cried.

There were times I would grow jealous
Because my mother is so far away.
But I realized I was being zealous
Making an unprovoked display.
You would tell me not to despair
That my mom was also my dearest friend

With a smile you would then declare
For a moment I'd gone round the bend.
If there was something we wanted to do
Your mother usually took precedence.
You were her son through and through
A princely child loved in decadence.

As a son I can say there is no other
Love that is greater than the love of a mother.

Early Mornings

In the early hours of morning while others were sleeping, David was often awake. He worked odd hours that required him to rise before the sun. In those tranquil moments when the world is quiet and calm, he was busy bustling about in anticipation of a long road trip or a day spent on his knees inventorying bulk items in a hot grocery store. His was an exhausting job which he hated but he loved early rising.

The early mornings brought David peace in an otherwise maddening occupation that taxed his body and broke his spirit. Day after day he would tell me how much he wanted to quit the inventory business and have a new adventure. He would contemplate his future as the sun would rise and ask himself what exactly was his ultimate desire. He wished to be a writer, to put his thoughts down on paper in a sensible way. He wanted to be cinema critic, analyzing each film to which he bore witness with his expertise in the arts of staging, lighting, sound, and quality of acting skills.

David desperately desired a life of note, one worthy of his gracious demeanor and peaceful disposition. He wanted to be a scholar or a school man or a person of great importance. He entertained ideas of political aspirations but could never convince himself to take part in the corruption of politics. There no devil like one in a suit.

Each morning that he woke before the dawn was another to remind him of his circumstances and force him to become introspective. He dreamed of the day when he could tell his job to shove it and sojourn to a life of meaning, a life dedicated to kindness and compassion. His was a mind filled with wonder at what the world could become and he cared deeply about the suffering of others. It was his destiny to give everything he could and to receive very little in recompense. A martyr who died without realizing his dreams. But I refuse to believe he felt only sorrow and know that his contemplative and meditative moments gave him great satisfaction on each and every early morning.

Pinterest and Twitter

David was obsessed with Pinterest and Twitter. He would stare at them both all day. Each represented a connection to the outside world he felt he lost somewhere along the way. He had something like 400 followers though he rarely pinned to his wall. I don't think I ever saw him tweet. He was the penultimate epitome of a modern-minded voyeur.

His obsession was focused upon the perfection of the human form, on the contours and characteristics of the naked male body. It was his pleasure to be a man who appreciated the artistic value of erotic images. He was truly interested in flesh as the absolute embodiment of beauty on earth. He was a man who looked to men as mirrors for his own inner beauty, his own flawed but attractive form.

The tweeting and the pinning and the posting and the poking were never of interest to David, at least not in taking an assertive or dominant role. His pleasure was to be submissive and to enjoy the conversations of others without engaging with them directly. In the cyber world of social media, David was a ghost. His avatar, his digital persona, stood in those binary worlds as an invisible figure, a nonentity concerned only with the capturing of special moments, through the adoration of a young beauty or the intellectual titillation of conversations carried into the cyber world in the form of status updates, posted to a hypothetic wall which is really a pattern of indecipherable codes.

I never saw David shy away from the chance to socialize with someone who intrigued him. He grew to be an extrovert in his last golden years but a part of him missed his former days as an introverted spectator, a quiet watcher standing idly amongst the masses to witness spectacular events. The passive part of David sought solace in social media, finding an outlet for his harmless voyeurism and desire to attain knowledge purely through speculation.

His was a heart that yearned for connection but his mind was interested in the pure peace of purposeful passivity.

<u>War</u>

Purity of love
Negates the fear and loathing
Leading men to war.

Goodbye

I still remember the day you saved my life
That day in the light of the summer sun
When your dulcet tones ended my strife,
When you exclaimed I was the one...

The one you'd been waiting to tell all you knew,
The one who'd be your most trusted friend,
A pagan father to lead me right on through
The darkness I thought had no end...

You said there was no place for me to hide
From the person I really should be.
With the goddess and god I was allied
The greatest power laid within me...

Your true name was Gwyn Beiciwr
And you said mine was Tân Plentyn
You taught me the power to conquer my fear
Showed kindness can erase any sin...

Your greatest law was to never be violent
And your three principles since the dawn were
To know, to dare, and to remember to
Always be silent...

Episcopacy

I once made the mistake of saying the Episcopal Church was a member of the Orthodoxy when standing in David's presence and he commenced to teach me a lesson.

"The church of my blood is not orthodox," he said, "It is the child of the Anglican Communion. The forefathers of my forefathers were brought into the folds of the Church of England after being expelled as heretic Huguenots from the kingdom of France." I didn't see the importance of his statement. I believed all Christian sects to be the same.

David had long ago left behind the faith of his family in exchange for the Deep Mysteries that came before but his passion in remembrance for the church of his birth was a point of pleasure for his nostalgia and longing to return.

The Anglican Communion began under the reign of Henry VIII when his conscience and cuckolded spirit led him to break from the fineries and corruption of the Catholics. The iconography of the Orthodoxy remained which is what led to my confusion. Yet the spirit of the church was changed. The protestant fire sparked by Calvin and Luther provided the cloth and the dogmas of orthodoxy were the needle.

David had no use for confession and preferred to avoid revivals in a tent. He found both to be wholly foreign. For that small part of him that remained Christian after his earthen conversion, the episcopacy was the place in which he wished to be. His life, which could've been longer, was devoted to the duties of a saint and a son. If any man was worthy of praise and recognition it was he. Through the canon rites of our Mysteries he is Saint David the Anglican.

I would urge each of us to follow in David's fashion, no matter which faith to which we subscribe. The point is not which sect you follow or whose authority is greater. The central concept of the Deep Mysteries which David held to be dear was: "Each person is free to form their own faith, in their own time, and by their own means. It is not the right of the temporal to pass judgment in the name of the spiritual." David was sure that all religions are the same.

Freedom

Freedom is not free.
It is a commodity
That comes with a cost.

Volcanoes

He would defend both the sinner and saint,
He never asked for rewards in return.
The world was a blank canvas that he'd paint,
Life a scented candle for him to burn.

Like a wolf howling at the waxing moon
His spirit danced in the land of new dreams.
He followed the ancient code of the rune
And knew nothing is ever as it seems.

His creed was one of perpetual peace
While his gods were of Avalon and the like
But if he was provoked he would not cease
Until he landed the last fatal strike.

His passion was unyieldingly abrupt,
As violent as when volcanoes erupt.

The Wise Man

A wise man knows when not to speak
That knowledge is the ultimate power to seek
That ignorance is what makes people weak.

A wise man knows all the ways to behave
That not all men are his mission to save
That sometimes you cannot avoid the wave.

A wise man knows what laws to enact
That truth is often times hard to extract
That only nature is matter of fact.

A wise man knows to avoid all stress
That insults cause men to digress
That patience is a virtue to possess.

A wise man knows how to perceive
That selfish people tend to deceive
That to make it real you must believe.

A wise man knows losing can be for the best
That sometimes failing is passing the test
That the only reprieve comes with eternal rest.

A wise man knows the depths of his heart
That the best fight is one that doesn't start
That all you can do in life is play your part.

A wise man knows passion is a gift
That jealousy will always cause a rift
That impatience causes the soul to drift.

A wise man knows to avoid a dead-end
That hubris often tends to offend
That humility is a man's dearest friend.

A wise man knows to teach without bias
That a master of religion is never pious
That the opinions of others can often try us.

You were a wise man, Mister Brew.
And all my wisdom I learned from you...

About the Author...

R.J. Pommarane is the author of *The Body Chaotic* and *The Tales of Albion Trilogy*. He is a scholar of language and history, having earned a BA in English from Portland State University before continuing on to pursue a MA in Education. R.J. is a follower of the Deep Mysteries, currently residing in Portland, Oregon, with his two cats, Kristopher and Shadow, and his partner, Kevin.

www.ingramcontent.com/pod-product-compliance
Lightning Source LLC
Chambersburg PA
CBHW071457070426
42452CB00040B/1555